WILDLIFE IN BLOOM SERIES

Little Owl

BY AUTHOR & CONSERVATIONIST

LINDA BLACKMOOR

ISBN: 978-1-966417-06-4 (PRINT)

PUBLISHED BY QUILL PRESS. LINDA BLACKMOOR'S TITLES MAY BE PURCHASED IN BULK FOR EDUCATIONAL, BUSINESS, FUNDRAISING, OR SALES PROMOTIONAL USE. FOR INFORMATION, PLEASE EMAIL HELLO@LINDABLACKMOOR.COM

FIRST PRINT EDITION: 2024

LINDA BLACKMOOR
WWW.LINDABLACKMOOR.COM

SPECIES

Owls belong to the order Strigiformes, with over 200 species found worldwide except in Antarctica. They range from the tiny Elf Owl, just 5 inches tall, and the majestic Blakiston's Fish Owl, boasting a wingspan up to 6.6 feet, to the magical Snowy Owl. Owls inhabit diverse environments including forests, deserts, mountains, and grasslands.

EYES

Owls have large, forward-facing eyes that provide excellent night vision and depth perception. Their eyes are fixed in their sockets, so they must rotate their heads up to 270 degrees to look around. Packed with rod cells sensitive to low light, their eyes allow them to see in near darkness. A special reflective layer called the tapetum lucidum enhances their night vision by reflecting light back through the retina.

HEARING

Possessing exceptional hearing, owls have asymmetrical ear placement that helps them pinpoint the exact location of sounds. Some species can detect the faint movements of prey under leaves or snow, even in complete darkness. Their facial discs act like satellite dishes, funneling sound waves to their ears for better detection. This acute hearing complements their vision, making them masterful nocturnal hunters.

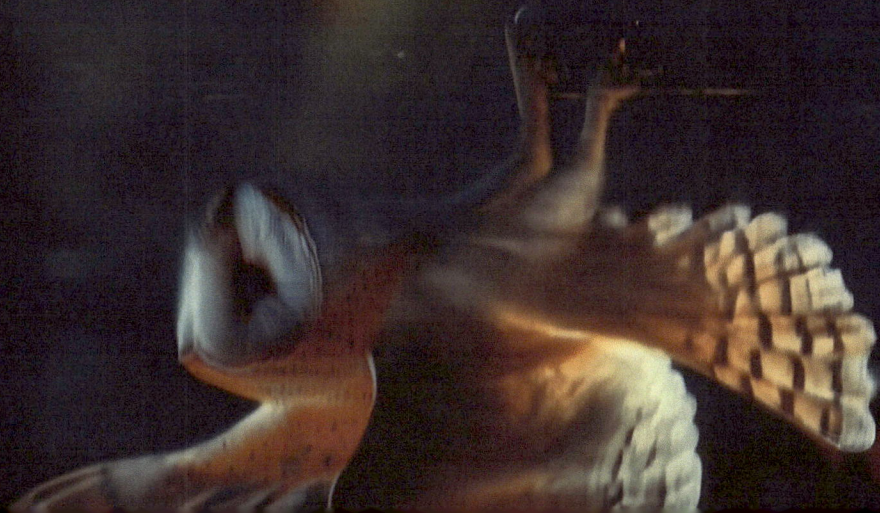

FLIGHT

Owls fly silently thanks to specialized feathers that reduce noise, allowing them to sneak up on prey. The edges of their flight feathers are fringed with tiny serrations called fimbriae, which break up air turbulence. This adaptation muffles the sound of air passing over their wings as they fly. Silent flight is essential for their hunting success and sets them apart from other birds of prey.

TALONS

Equipped with sharp talons, owls are skilled predators capable of capturing prey swiftly. Their feet have a unique arrangement called zygodactyl, with two toes facing forward and two backward, providing a strong grip. This foot structure helps them seize prey and perch securely on branches. Their powerful talons are vital tools for hunting and survival.

OWL FACTS #6

DIET

Owls are carnivorous, feeding on rodents, insects, fish, and other small animals, playing a vital role in controlling pest populations. They swallow small prey whole and later regurgitate pellets containing indigestible materials like bones and fur. Studying these pellets helps scientists understand owl diets and local ecosystems. Their hunting helps maintain ecological balance in their habitats.

NECK

Owls can rotate their heads up to 270 degrees due to special adaptations in their bones and blood vessels. They have 14 neck vertebrae, more than most birds, allowing remarkable flexibility. Special blood vessels ensure blood flow to the brain isn't cut off when they turn their heads. This ability compensates for their fixed eye position and enhances their field of vision.

CAMO

Owl feathers often have patterns and colors that provide excellent camouflage, helping them blend into their surroundings. This camouflage protects them from predators and aids in ambushing prey. Some species, like the Eastern Screech Owl, resemble tree bark when at rest during the day. Effective camouflage is crucial for their survival in the wild.

NESTING

Owls typically nest in tree cavities, abandoned nests of other birds, or on cliffs, laying 1 to 13 eggs depending on the species. The female incubates the eggs while the male provides food, ensuring the family's well-being. Owlets hatch after about a month and are cared for by both parents as they grow rapidly. They learn to hunt and fly before becoming independent.

VOCALS

Owls communicate using a variety of vocalizations such as hoots, screeches, whistles, and barks unique to each species. These calls are used for mating, defending territory, and communicating between mates and offspring. Their vocalizations can be heard over long distances, especially at night when they are most active. Communication is essential for their social interactions and survival.

OWL FACTS #11

HABITAT

Owls inhabit a wide range of habitats including forests, deserts, grasslands, and tundra, adapting to various climates and environments. They are found on every continent except Antarctica, showcasing their remarkable adaptability. Some species prefer dense woodlands, while others thrive in open plains or near water bodies. Their ability to live in diverse habitats highlights their resilience.

OWL FACTS #12

PELLETS

Owls regurgitate pellets composed of indigestible materials like bones, fur, and feathers from their prey. These pellets provide valuable information about their diet and local prey species. Scientists and students often dissect owl pellets to study food chains and understand ecosystem dynamics. This behavior is an important aspect of owl biology and ecology.

TUFTS

Some owls have distinctive ear tufts, which are feathers that stick up on their heads but aren't related to hearing. Species like the Great Horned Owl and the Long-eared Owl display these tufts, which may help with camouflage by breaking up their outline among tree branches. The tufts can also express the owl's mood —standing erect when alert or laying flat when relaxed.

www.ingramcontent.com/pod-product-compliance
Lightning Source LLC
Chambersburg PA
CBHW060838270326

41933CB00002B/120